P9-CKK-613

A PORTFOLIO OF

LANDSCAPING
IDEAS

CREATIVE
PUBLISHING
international

MINNETONKA, MINNESOTA

www.howtobookstore.com

CONTENTS

What Makes Great Landscaping?....... 4

Planning........................... 6

Determining Your Needs............. 8

  Budget....................... 10

  Size & Contour of Your Yard..... 12

  Private Space.................. 14

  Function of Your Yard......... 16

Designing Your Yard........... 18

  Materials............... 20

  Composition & Color.......... 24

  Personal Style............... 26

A Portfolio of Landscaping Ideas..... 28

  Patios & Porches.............. 30

  Decks....................... 34

  Retaining Walls............... 38

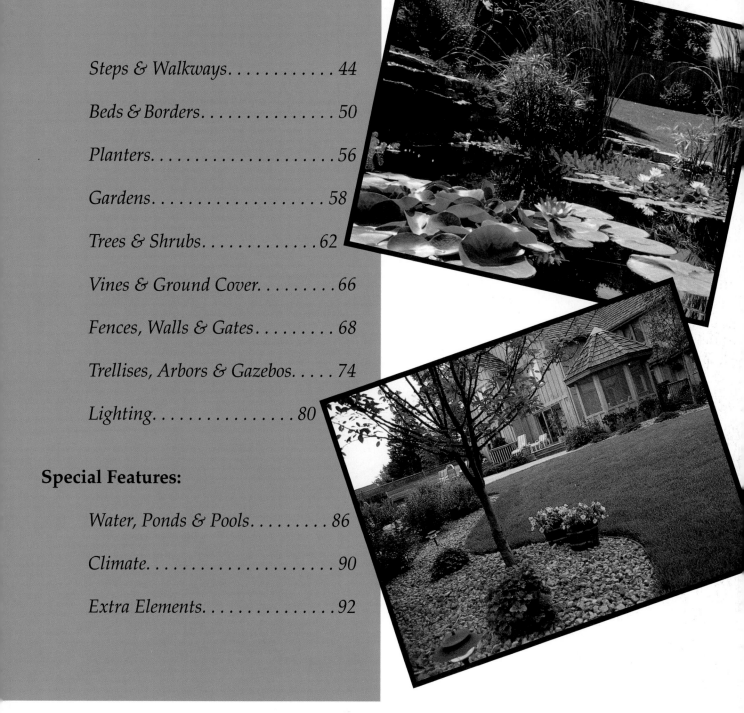

Steps & Walkways. 44

Beds & Borders. 50

Planters. 56

Gardens. 58

Trees & Shrubs. 62

Vines & Ground Cover. 66

Fences, Walls & Gates. 68

Trellises, Arbors & Gazebos. 74

Lighting. 80

Special Features:

Water, Ponds & Pools. 86

Climate. 90

Extra Elements. 92

© Copyright 1994
Creative Publishing international, Inc.
5900 Green Oak Drive
Minnetonka, Minnesota 55343
1-800-328-3895
www.howtobookstore.com
All rights reserved

Printed by R.R. Donnelly & Sons Co.
10 9 8 7 6 5 4 3

President/CEO: David D. Murphy
Executive V.P./Editor-in-Chief: Patricia K. Jacobsen
Vice President/Retail Sales & Marketing: Richard M. Miller

Cover photo (top right) courtesy of Weatherend Estate Furniture.

Author: Home How-To Institute™
Creative Director: William B. Jones
Project Director: Paul Currie
Art Director: Geoffrey Kinsey
Project Manager: Kristen Olson
Writers: Stacy Sheagley, Carol Harvatin
Copy Editor: Janice Cauley
Production Staff: Geoffrey Kinsey,
  Julie Sutphen
Vice President of Development
  Planning & Production: Jim Bindas
Production Manager: Linda Halls

Library of Congress
Cataloging-in-Publication Data

Portfolio of landscaping.
p. cm.

ISBN 0-86573-940-4 (softcover)
1. Landscape gardening. 2. Landscape architecture.
I. Cy DeCosse Incorporated.
SB473.P63 1994
712-dc20   94-20074

WHAT MAKES GREAT LANDSCAPING?

Great landscaping is a work of art. Think of your yard as a picture that is created using aspects of design, such as line, form and color, in the same way an artist uses them. The picture your landscape creates is a reflection of who you are and what you like. We have included over 140 color photographs of great landscaping designs in *A Portfolio of Landscaping Ideas* to help you plan a landscape that fits your taste and needs.

Landscaping can serve many functions, such as helping to control sunlight, wind or a sloped yard that may be eroding. A newly built home that is bare of grass or trees offers the chance to create a landscape exactly the way you want. With careful planning, you can create an outdoor space that is beautiful and

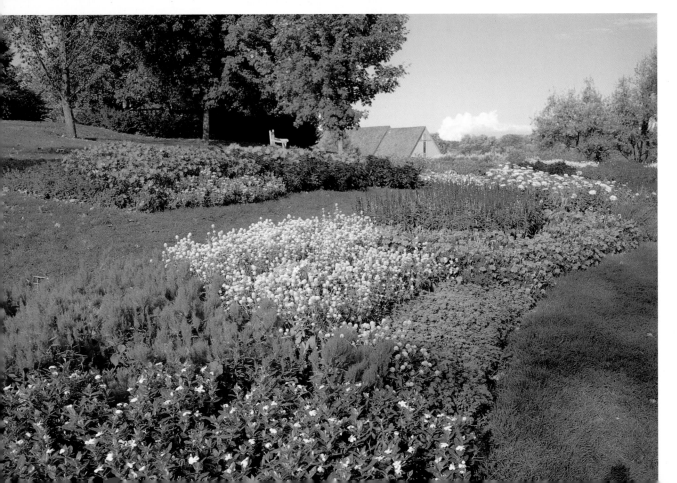

functional. You can use landscaping to create additional living space outdoors or to provide privacy for your existing outdoor space. A beautifully landscaped yard increases the value of your property by enhancing the attractiveness of your home and making it more inviting.

A Portfolio of Landscape Ideas will help you create a landscape that is ideally suited to you and your yard. We begin by helping you determine your landscape needs and what type of yard you have. You will also need to know the budget you are working with. To help you design your personal landscape, this book includes a portfolio of photographs of beautifully landscaped yards. Here you will find ideas for patios, porches, decks, walkways, trees, shrubs, plants, enclosures and lighting to inspire you and help you plan a landscape design that best fulfills your specific requirements. There are even ideas for dealing with special landscaping needs, such as water, climate and unusual or unusable space in your yard.

You don't need to be an expert to create a beautiful and satisfying yard. Whether you do the work yourself or hire someone to do it for you, you will still need to spend time planning if you want your landscape to serve specific functions. This book will help you design a landscape that will allow you to enjoy the fruits of your labor for years to come.

This photo and opposite page (top) courtesy of Bachman's Landscaping Service. Sue Hartley, photography.

Photo courtesy of Dundee Nursery

PLANNING

Before you begin landscaping, you need to plan the project. This includes deciding not only what type of yard you want to have, but how much money you can spend. You must take into consideration the area you are living in: who are your neighbors and what are their yards like? You will be making choices, not only about design, but about types of materials and how much they cost. If you want to include more elaborate features, you might have to scale back in one area in order to emphasize another that is more important to you. Working these decisions out in the beginning will help you avoid problems later on in the project, saving time and expense. Landscaping your yard is a fun and exciting project that needs time for preparation but also lets you create the yard you've always wanted.

Photo courtesy of Bachman's Landscaping Service. Sue Hartley, photography.

Teakwood Garden Furniture by Barlow Tyrie

Photo courtesy of Norby & Associates, Inc.

DETERMINING YOUR NEEDS

What kind of landscaping design suits your personal needs and style? If you have a growing family, you will probably want to include a playground and maybe empty yard space for active games. If you are an avid gardener, you will want your yard to include areas for growing flowers or vegetables. Perhaps you have always wanted a yard with exotic features, such as a fountain or a small gazebo. This is the time to consider your favorite outdoor environments and how you might recreate them in your own yard.

Photo courtesy of Anchor Wall Systems, Inc.

Photo courtesy of California Redwood Association

Photo courtesy of Southern Pine Council

DETERMINING YOUR NEEDS
Budget

Budget is your first determining factor in landscape design. A small budget will of course limit the extent of your design, but not the ability to create interesting areas within your yard. Be prepared to purchase materials such as wood, stone and/or brick as well as plants such as trees, shrubs and/or flowers. Some of the structures you might be building include fences, decks, trellises and patios; you will also want to consider planters, walkways and steps. Researching the cost of materials before you begin the actual work will help you make sure your plans fit your budget.

Carefully considering your taste and needs as well as your existing yard space will eliminate problems in the future and give you a head start in designing the best landscape possible. Note the difference in expense but not in resulting styles in the following photos.

Photo courtesy of Terry Tempus; TCT Landscaping

A brick walkway lined with shade-loving plants leads to a tranquil hot tub enclosure. The materials used to build this enclosure were not particularly expensive, but special design elements like the windows shown here can add to your costs.

Photo courtesy of Dundee Nursery

This suburban home has a young, fairly inexpensive landscape. A cluster of small shrubs and a young tree are featured on one side of the front walk. Brilliant red salvia provides balance and color on the other side of the walk. These plants will continue to grow and fill this space. Adding a few new plantings each year is an inexpensive way to continue to increase the value of your landscape.

Photo courtesy of Bachman's Landscaping Service. Sue Hartley, photography.

Round concrete pavers with a unique texture were used to create a pathway that leads from one area of the yard to another. Small, inexpensive elements like these pavers are a great way to add an interesting visual accent to your landscape at a reasonable cost.

DETERMINING YOUR NEEDS

Size & Contour of Your Yard

Determining your needs includes looking realistically at the yard space available to you. Is it small or large, square or unusually shaped? What are the natural elements you have to contend with? Does it have many trees? Consider how large they are and how old. Note which parts of your yard receive the most sun and from which direction. Be prepared to work with your yard and not against it. You can turn unusual features into points of interest and divide a basic square yard into unique shapes with distinctive lines and characteristics.

Natural elements are used to define the boundaries of this rolling, open lawn. The open grass area can be used for outdoor activities or large gatherings. Neatly landscaped areas help define the boundaries of the yard, yet still maintain the feeling of wide-open spaces. Tall, well-shaped evergreens and several smaller bushes create a border at the back of the yard and give the space some privacy.

Retaining walls can create usable space in areas that would otherwise remain unused. This wall provides large planting areas for bushes, flowering plants and even a small tree. The interlocking blocks complement the brickwork of the house and help to unify the landscape.

This photo and all on opposite page courtesy of Bachman's Landscaping Service. Sue Hartley, photography.

A large house and accompanying yard demand an equally large landscape. Here several varieties of tall trees have been planted in strategic places within the landscape. The large trees balance the size of the structure and soften its sharp angles. Flowers in front of the house add color and elegance.

The stately elegance of this house is reflected in the graceful landscape that surrounds it. Well-manicured hedges combine with benches to frame small beds of white impatiens. Their crisp square angles are also reflected in the open, square design of the deck and the way it frames the neatly trimmed grass. The expansive rolling lawn helps to balance the house and serves as a natural extension of the deck area.

Photo courtesy of Dundee Nursery

13

DETERMINING YOUR NEEDS

Private Space

You will also need to consider factors such as your desire for privacy. City dwellers find privacy in short commodity and often long for an enclosed, secluded area with obvious boundaries. Fencing is the obvious choice for creating these private areas, and the amount of privacy desired will determine what type of fencing is used. Landscapes that don't have such a demand for privacy might include less enclosed structures like open-walled gazebos, arbors and trellises. Refer to local codes when building landscape structures for specifics such as legal fence heights, required setbacks from property lines and other code issues. For safety reasons, consult with local utility companies before you start any outdoor construction.

Photo courtesy of Terry Tempus, TCT Landscaping. This photo and the one below left courtesy of Bachman's Landscaping Service. Sue Hartley, photography.

A solid brick-and-wood fence gives character and privacy to this quiet setting. The brick adds interest to the fence and coordinates with the stone pavers and small boulders and stones bordering the pond.

A private area was created by building terraced retaining walls into a steep slope. The wooden retaining walls provide a place for vertical flower gardens and planting beds.

Lush green trees and shrubs create a beautiful, living visual boundary and give this open patio area some needed privacy. With a living privacy fence, however, your privacy may be diminished when the leaves fall.

DETERMINING YOUR NEEDS

Function of Your Yard

As you begin the process of designing your yard, consider your favorite activities and personal taste. If you love to entertain, you might want to include patio space large enough for parties and lots of outdoor lights for nighttime events. If you wish for solitude, you can create private corners shaded from the rest of the yard or interesting walkways that lead to unexpected areas. Nature lovers might wish for a yard that replicates the freedom of the country and has lots of room for wildflowers and wildlife.

Even if your yard is small, you can create miniature environments that provide a sense of your own style and satisfy your needs. If your time is limited, you might want to design a yard that requires little maintenance but still allows you to enjoy the outdoors. Terraces, fences and other structures add interesting lines and textures to a landscape while serving a practical purpose.

Photo courtesy of Norby & Associates, Inc.

Large beds of multicolored impatiens lead the way to a swimming pool tucked away on a wooded hill. Lush greenery surrounding the pool creates a smooth transition from pool to yard and gives pool users a scenic landscape to enjoy.

Photo courtesy of Kristine Distel & Associates Landscaping

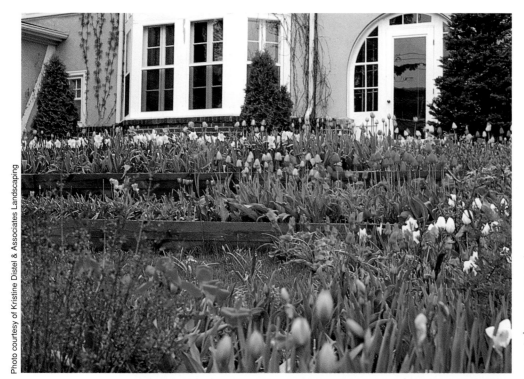

An impressive tulip bed creates a sea of red, white, yellow and pink that brightens the house and fills the yard with color in early spring. Later, when the bulbs are finished blooming, flowering annuals will be planted among the bulbs to continue the colorful theme throughout the season.

A separate niche was created in this deck with built-in benches and integrated flower boxes. Colorful annuals overflow from the planters to frame this intimate alcove.

Photo courtesy of Southern Pine Council. © Larry Payne.

17

DESIGNING YOUR YARD

Designing your yard is fun and exciting. This is where you actually put your plans and ideas on paper. It is a good idea to draw your yard as it is now, including the house and any other features that will be retained or are important, such as where the sun hits, where the neighbors are located and what the view is from particular areas. Include trouble spots, such as eroded slopes, areas that receive little rain and places where noise or litter are a problem. Take a walk around the neighborhood, noting which

yards appeal to you and any elements they contain that you would like to include in your own design.

When designing your yard, remember to leave lots of room around plants for future growth. Draw any structures you would like to include, noting the types of material they will be made from and size and location relative to other areas of the yard, in order to maintain a balanced and integrated look.

Photo courtesy of Holm & Olson, Inc.

Photo courtesy of Kristine Distel & Associates Landscaping

Photo courtesy of Anderson Design Services, Ltd.

DESIGNING YOUR YARD

Materials

Stone, masonry and wood are primary building materials for landscape construction. Stone and masonry give your landscape structures a feeling of permanence. Wood has a natural, warm look, is easy to shape and can be painted or stained to match existing structures.

Whenever possible, choose landscape materials that either match or complement the materials already used on your home. For example, if you have a brick home, a patio made from similar brick will be more appealing than a poured concrete slab. Or, if you have a Tudor-style house with exposed beams, a retaining wall built from rough timbers is more appropriate than a wall built from interlocking concrete blocks.

Man-made stone products cast from concrete are a good choice for landscape structures, considering the increasing price and dwindling supplies of forest timber and natural stone. Interlocking concrete block, brick pavers and other manufactured stone products are widely available, easy to install and very durable.

If you prefer the look of natural stone, try to select a type of rock that is common to your geographic region. Local stone makes your landscape look natural, and it is much less expensive than stone that must be shipped long distances.

Interlocking block (below) is made from molded concrete that is split to provide a rough face resembling natural stone. Available in several colors and sizes, interlocking block is used for both straight and curved retaining walls, terraces and raised planting beds. Interlocking block walls create bold geometric patterns.

Concrete block is available in plain or decorative types. This durable building material is used often for free-standing garden walls. The hard, plain look of a concrete block wall can be softened with climbing plants or a surface application of stucco or stone veneer.

Poured concrete is durable and less expensive than other paving products. Although concrete is plain in appearance, it is easy to maintain, making it a popular choice for walkways, patios, walls and steps.

Interlocking pavers made from molded concrete are used in patios, walkways and driveways. Available in a variety of colors and shapes, interlocking pavers are a good way to add distinctive patterns to a landscape.

Brick is an elegant, traditional building material made from molded, oven-dried clay. Available in many styles, brick is used to build patios, walkways, edging and free-standing garden walls.

Terra cotta and adobe are molded clay products that are dried in the sun. They are used for patios, walkways and garden walls. These products have a porous surface that can be damaged by water, so terra cotta and adobe are best suited for very dry climates.

Concrete pavers are made from poured concrete and are available in many decorative shapes, textures and colors. Inexpensive and easy to install, concrete pavers are used for patios, walkways and steps.

21

Crushed gravel

Smooth river gravel

Cut stone (granite)

Flagstone

Glacial rubble stone

Accent rock (quartz blend)

Natural Stone

Gravel comes in two forms: rough gravel made by crushing larger rocks, and smooth gravel usually dredged from rivers. Gravel is sorted by size, and has many landscape uses. Applied as a loose layer, gravel makes an informal, easy-to-maintain pathway. Laid in large beds, gravel lends a relaxed feeling to a landscape while providing texture and color.

Cut stone, sometimes called ashlar, is natural stone that has been cut into cubic shapes. Marble, hard limestone, and granite (shown here) are popular for cut stone. Cut stone is used for both mortared or unmortared walls, patios or walkways. It is an expensive, top-quality building material that gives landscape structures an elegant, timeless appearance.

Flagstone is uncut sedimentary stone that has naturally flat surfaces. Limestone, slate, and shale are common types of flagstone. Flagstone works well with large, expansive landscapes, and is used for walkways, patios, and steps. It is a durable, but expensive, paving material.

Rubble stone is any type of irregular, uncut rock collected from fields, gullies, or stream beds. It can include boulders, glacial debris, rough pieces of quartz or granite, random pieces of limestone or sandstone, or even volcanic rock. Rubble stone often is used in garden walls and retaining walls, and works best in informal, rustic landscapes. Rubble stone is cheaper than cut stone.

Accent rock is distinctive natural stone used as a decoration rather than as a building material. Large, colorful rocks can be partially buried in a planting area or lawn to add visual interest. Accent rocks can range from small 20-lb. pieces to enormous boulders weighing more than a ton.

Wood

Wood and bark chips are used for loose fill on soft pathways or as a ground cover for planting areas. Wood and bark chips are inexpensive and lend a relaxed, casual look to a landscape.

Pressure-treated pine contains pesticides and wood preservatives to make it last. Less expensive than cedar and redwood, pressure-treated pine is used to build fences, retaining walls, raised planting beds, and garden steps. Most pressure-treated pine is green when new, but gradually weathers to a neutral gray. Or, it can be stained to resemble redwood or cedar. In some areas, treated pine is also available in a dark-brown color.

Cedar is a soft wood with a rough texture. It has natural resistance to decay and insect damage, and is used for fences, trellises, and arbors. Use cedar in above-ground structures only: where wood will be in contact with the ground, use pressure-treated lumber instead.

Redwood is a smooth-grained wood with a natural resistance to insects and decay. It is used for above-ground structures, like fences, trellises, and overhead arbors. Avoid using redwood where a structure will be in contact with the ground: for these applications, use pressure-treated wood instead. Because of high demand and dwindling supplies, redwood is becoming more expensive.

Redwood bark chips

Pressure-treated pine

Wood chips

Cedar

Redwood

DESIGNING YOUR YARD

Composition & Color

Composition is an aspect of landscaping that includes the use of scale, line, color and material as well as elements such as focal points and sun versus shade. Consider the composition of your yard as you study your design. Is it balanced? Is color attractively placed throughout the landscape or is it limited to one area? Have you selected flowers and shrubs with varying blooming periods so you have constant color throughout the season? Do the objects you have included complement each other in size and texture, or do they clash? Repetition of color, shape and texture helps to unify a landscape and give your yard a well-groomed, elegant look.

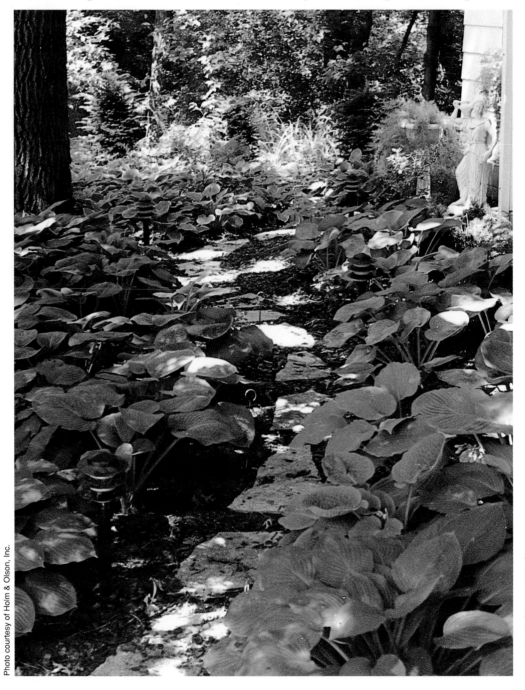

Photo courtesy of Holm & Olson, Inc.

A narrow path of flagstone winds through a large bed of hostas. The large, elegant leaves of the hosta plants create a lush, green ground cover. Some hostas produce decorative spikes of flowers during blooming season, enhancing the landscape even more.

Photo courtesy of Anchor Wall Systems, Inc.

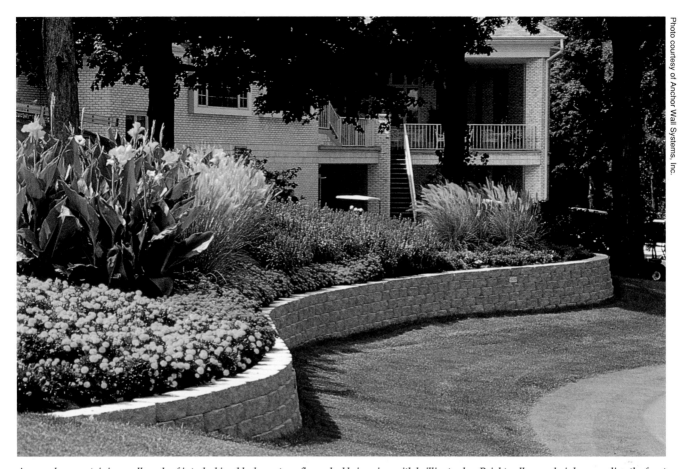

A curved gray retaining wall made of interlocking block creates a flower bed brimming with brilliant color. Bright yellow and pink mums line the front of the bed, while taller yellow calla lilies and ornamental grass create a colorful backdrop. Flowering salvia fills the rest of the bed with deep purple.

A small fountain adds movement and sound to this garden pond. Natural stones, ferns, grasses and waterlilies surround this pond to create a tranquil woodland setting and make it the focal point of the landscape.

Photo courtesy of Anderson Design Services, Ltd.

DESIGNING YOUR YARD

Personal Style

Keeping in mind the importance of what has been previously discussed, remember that landscaping is a personal choice, reflecting your own taste and sense of style. Choose colors and textures that are pleasing to you and a design that fits your nature. Some people will prefer large splashes of color while others will want their yard to reflect more subtle hues. Some will choose the rough texture of stone rather than concrete's smoother surface. An orderly landscape says something very different from one that is more "natural."

Include features in your yard that reflect your individuality. You don't have to rely on the "experts" to design a great landscape. Your landscape will be your own work of art and, above all else, should provide personal satisfaction for years to come.

This photo and opposite page (bottom) courtesy of Bachman's Landscaping Service. Sue Hartley, photography.

The curved line of the rock-filled planting bed creates a soft edge as it meets the neatly trimmed lawn and gives a smooth, rolling feel to the entire landscape. The round edges of the bed reflect the round design used in the gazebo structure seen in the background. And the pink tint in the rock will match the blossoms of the crabapple tree.

To preserve the natural look of this setting, simple wood planks are used as a bridge over a small stream. This thick growth of trees, shrubs, grasses and ferns creates a lush woodland retreat.

Photo courtesy of Terry Tempus, TCT Landscaping

Photo courtesy of Dundee Nursery

Meticulously manicured European Privet hedges give symmetry and balance to this formal garden. The uniformly shaped hedges encompass flower beds filled with orderly rows of white impatiens. The white blossoms tie in with the white benches and birdbaths, and reinforce the pristine look of this stately landscape.

A multitude of flowering hostas and impatiens create a border of rich color in this shady area. A second variety of hosta planted around a tree introduces a new color while maintaining the overall theme of hostas and impatiens. Hostas are available in both green and variegated varieties.

A PORTFOLIO
of Landscaping Ideas

PATIOS & PORCHES

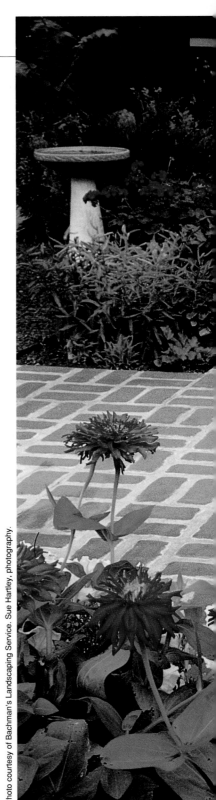

Patios and porches are outdoor rooms that are an extension of your house. They can be used for dining, entertaining or relaxing, and often act as a transition area between house and garden or other parts of the lawn. A terrace is a patio that is raised above the level of your main outdoor area and is used mainly when dealing with a sloped yard. The elevation of a terrace means it is visually prominent, so keep this in mind if you are planning to build one.

Materials used most often when building a porch or patio are wood, interlocking block, concrete block or poured concrete, bricks made from either terra cotta or adobe (made from molded clay and dried in the sun) and either concrete or interlocking pavers. Each of these materials provides a distinctive pattern and texture. When choosing your materials, remember that they should match or complement your home. Some are more expensive than others, and some adapt more easily to certain construction designs (poured concrete is more easily adapted to a curved area than other types of materials).

Photo courtesy of Osmose Wood Preserving, Inc.

Photo courtesy of Bachman's Landscaping Service. Sue Hartley, photography.

This ground-level deck with smooth, curved edges has low, wide-tiered steps leading to a patio level. Wooden benches and flower boxes filled with colorful annuals decorate the open deck and create a cozy outdoor sitting area. Raised garden beds are incorporated into this deck to provide more space for planting.

Brick, a traditional outdoor building material, sets a simple pattern for this modest patio. Brightly colored zinnias and petunias and a variety of green plants provide color as they separate the patio from the rest of the landscape.

A brick patio extends the living area of the home to the outdoors. A small raised deck that steps down to the patio provides the transition from indoor living area to the outdoor living area of the patio. Stately birch trees provide shade, yet keep the space bright and breezy.

All photos on these two pages courtesy of Dundee Nursery

This brick patio is a combination seating area and walkway. The curved lines in the brickwork create a smooth visual flow around the rounded planting areas. The planting beds are filled with a combination of flowering bushes, like the potentilla with white flowers; ground-spreading conifers, like the spreading juniper; and more delicate trees, like the birch, with its small limbs and white bark. A solid wood fence gives this backyard patio seclusion and privacy.

Varying the color of the brick in this patio makes it more casual and more visually interesting. The warm color of the brick is set off by white lawn furniture and colorful annuals. Small planting areas are incorporated into the design and filled with shrubs and flowers to brighten and soften this patio setting.

DECKS

Decks are a perfect way to expand your living space to the outdoors. They can either be connected to the house or built free-standing. The design you choose will depend on how you will be using it: for family get-togethers, a place to relax outdoors, a private area for sunbathing or even neighborhood dances. Often it includes a pool or hot tub. If you plan to entertain frequently, your deck should connect conveniently to the kitchen.

Photo courtesy of Bachman's Landscaping Service. Sue Hartley, photography.

This elaborate deck is surrounded by a steeply tiered retaining wall made of the same material as the deck. The main area provides lots of comfortable space that can be used for a variety of occasions. Built-in benches and a large planting box filled with colorful annuals define the edge of the single-level deck. The expansive retaining wall is planted with shrubs and flowering plants that will cover it with lush, living color when mature.

Photo courtesy of California Redwood Association

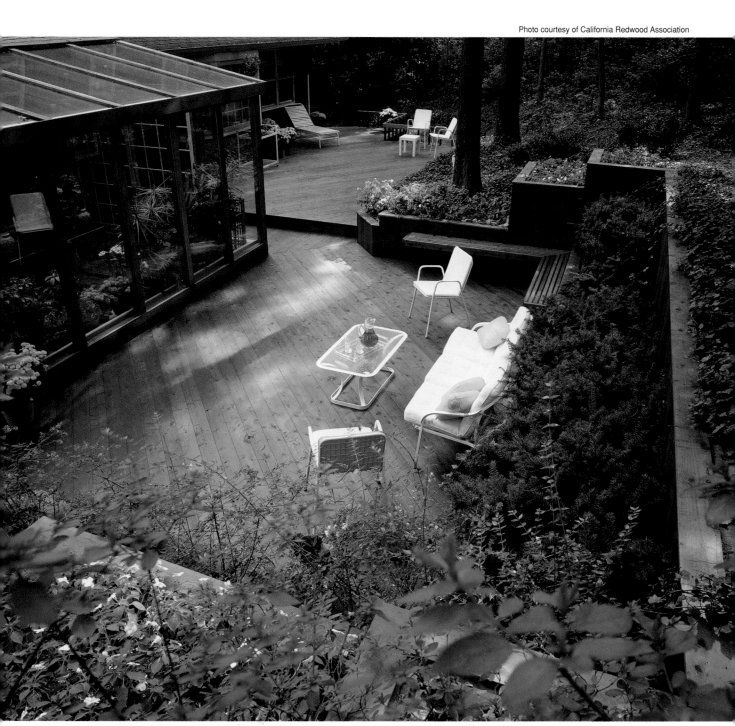

When this redwood deck is viewed from above, lush greenery fills the eye and a sense of undisturbed privacy emanates from below. This large deck features two separate areas, one section of which is built off a sunroom. A large wall made of planter boxes and built-in benches provides seclusion and privacy. The deck extends along the house and one step up leads to the second, more open area bordered by a low wall with built-in planter boxes.

This photo and opposite page (bottom) courtesy of Western Wood Products Association

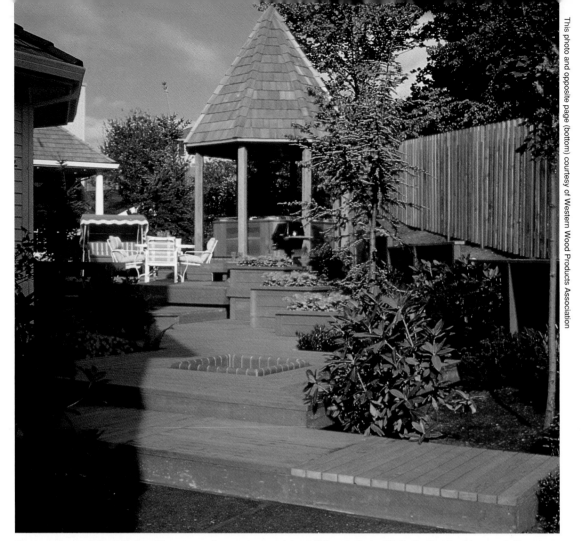

Here another multilevel deck, with many angles, creates a variety of different effects. While the first level is essentially a step to the next, the second level sports a square firepit and is surrounded by matching planters. A small level leads up to the top area which is used for dining. A gazebo built at one end provides shade and privacy.

Photo courtesy of California Redwood Association

Unusual curves give a distinctive air to this cantilevered redwood deck which was built on a slope over a wooded area. Nestled among the treetops, this redwood deck is large enough to hold a small table and two chairs on one side and a redwood bench with pillows for additional comfort on the other. Overhead, leafy trees form a sheltering canopy.

Photo courtesy of Anderson Design Services, Ltd.

An elegant white rail fence defines the lines of this deck as it angles out from the house and down to the yard. The clean, crisp look of the rail matches the design of the house and creates a theme that extends to the neatly manicured landscape.

This multilevel deck is built above level ground to accommodate a sunken firepit that is built into the lower level. The angles and lines of the decking pattern accent the square shape of the firepit. Bushes, flowering plants and ferns, planted in the yard, emerge around the edges of the deck to add color and greenery and to fill the space between the ground and the deck.

RETAINING WALLS

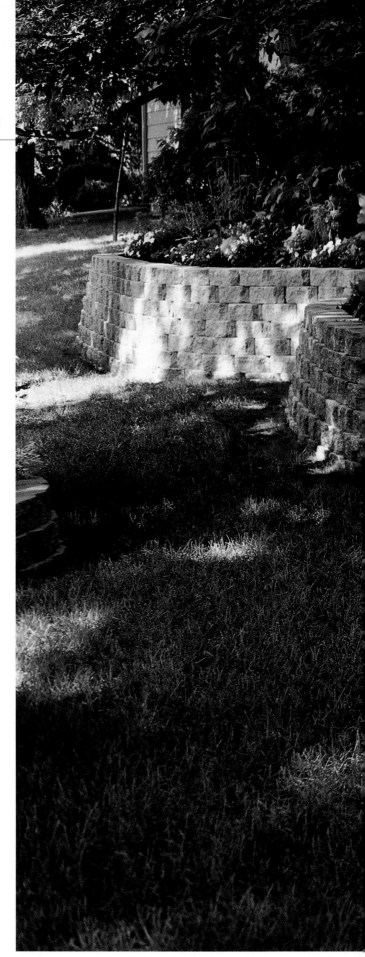

Retaining walls are generally used to manage slopes that limit usable outdoor space and also create an erosion problem. Effectively dealing with the problem of erosion, they are also visually pleasing, giving them a dual purpose. Hillsides make it difficult to plant and mow grass or raise other shrubs, plants and flowers. Terraces, two or more retaining walls used for the same slope, have flat areas between them, providing additional growing space, and are useful for slopes that are especially steep.

Materials used for retaining walls are interlocking blocks, stones and timber in a variety of styles. These materials add color, shape and texture to a yard and are sturdy enough to support the weight they must bear. The type of material you choose will depend on finances as well as on the amount of time you wish to invest in your yard. Timbers are easily placed on top of each other and held together with spikes, while stones and interlocking blocks need to be carefully aligned and are generally more expensive.

This handsome retaining wall, made of interlocking blocks, adds shape and texture to the yard. The raised flower beds provide color and are safe from damage caused by traffic or active use of the yard.

Photo courtesy of Anchor Wall Systems, Inc.

Rubble stones and large boulders are used for this retaining wall, which has been built to manage a slope at the perimeter of the yard. Enough flat space has been left between the wall and the fence to plant several trees and shrubs, while flowers and ground cover have been tucked into niches between the stones.

These photos and opposite page (top) courtesy of Bachman's Landscaping Service. Sue Hartley, photography.

This close-up of a rubble stone retaining wall shows how ground cover, artistically planted, can soften the stones' rough edges and provide bursts of color that stand out against the gray, rough texture of the stone.

Here a steep slope has been managed by building high timber retaining walls. Matching timber steps extend from the wall and lead up to the top of the slope. Small shrubs and flowering bushes are planted along the wall and on top of one level. When mature, these plants will cover and soften the angles and edges of this expansive retaining wall.

This retaining wall is built of rounded timbers and has been attractively draped with creeping ground cover. The deep green of the ground cover helps the wall to blend harmoniously with the wooded landscape behind it.

Photo courtesy of Dundee Nursery

Here another steep slope is transformed into a beautiful background for an outdoor deck area by building several terraced walls that have been planted with lush greenery. At the bottom of the wall a built-in bench helps make the transition to the deck area. A large built-in planting box overflows with colorful annuals. The fence at the top provides safety while distinctly separating the lawn from the rest of the space.

This photo and opposite page courtesy of Bachman's Landscaping Service. Sue Hartley, photography.

This timber retaining wall peeks out between the mature hosta and spirea plants surrounding it. The plants and trees have created an appealing still life that uses the wall as its background. Rocks, large and small, provide extra texture and break up the blend of greenery.

Photo courtesy of Anchor Wall Systems, Inc.

This small, curved retaining wall highlights the two trees it encircles. Pink impatiens and purple salvia fill the empty space around the trees with soft color. The wall provides a distinctive landscaping element by adding interesting shape and texture to the area.

STEPS & WALKWAYS

Steps are used for ascending a sloped yard and need to be level and easy to climb. Walkways are like "hallways" leading from one yard area or "room" to another. They help to direct traffic and are often an extension of steps. While steps are usually built from flagstone, brick, timbers, concrete block or poured concrete, walkways can be made from loose materials, such as rock or bark, for areas with light traffic flow, or from stone, brick or poured concrete for more heavily trafficked areas.

Curved walkways give a softened look to a landscape, while sharp lines and angles fit well with contemporary styles. The shape and type of material you use for your steps and/or walkway should complement both your house and the rest of your yard. Keep in mind color, texture and line when designing this part of your landscape.

Photo courtesy of Bachman's Landscaping Service. Sue Hartley, photography.

Circular stones (left) make a small walkway across a pebbled bed leading from grass to a stone path. The curves add a unique shape to this landscape, providing a point of interest.

This curving walkway (right) is made of brick surrounded by beds of stone and small shrubs. The end of the path turns into matching brick steps leading down a slope. Wooden steps above connect the house to the path.

Photo courtesy of Dundee Nursery

Red brick steps lead from the sidewalk to the top of this small hill and the house behind it. The bricks match those in the house and add interesting texture and color, making them the focal point in this landscape. Matching bright red geraniums in planters stand on either side of the steps.

Photo courtesy of Kristine Distel & Associates Landsca

Photo courtesy of Dundee Nursery

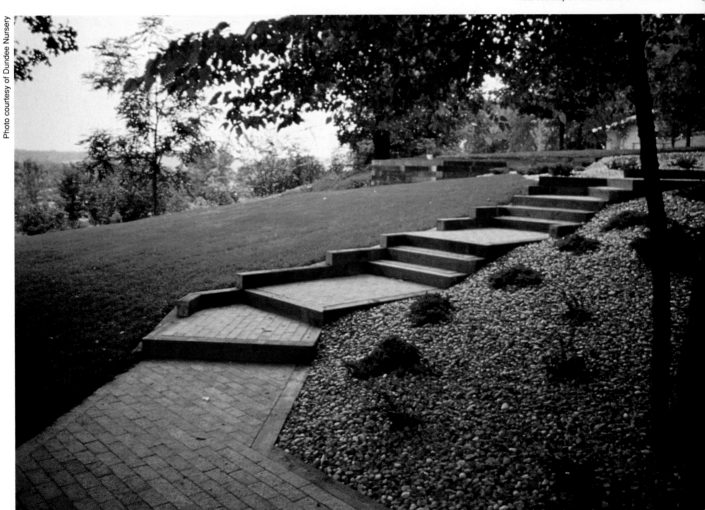

These angular steps, although not all the same length, are unified by their similarity in depth and material. Wooden edging connects the different shapes while the various lines themselves work together to create sharp definition and interesting corners.

46

Photo courtesy of Norby & Associates, Inc.

Here a steep slope has been managed with wooden steps leading through rock retaining walls. The two textures, wood and rock, go well with each other and with the surrounding landscape of trees, ferns, bushes and wood chips covering the ground.

This curved walkway extends from the driveway to the front door and is lined with red brick to match the house and garage. A variety of annuals, shrubs and trees border the walkway, while gravel is used to fill in the beds. The overall effect is neat and symmetrical without appearing artificial.

Photo courtesy of Bachman's Landscaping Service. Sue Hartley, photography.

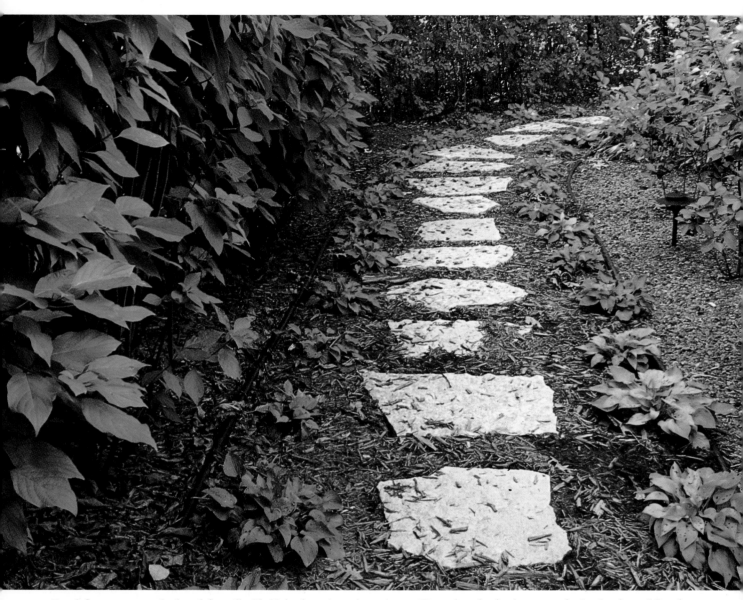

Rough flagstone, unevenly shaped, fits well with this landscape's rustic appearance. Hosta plants border the stone, softening its edges, while cedar chips provide color and weed control. Although the effect looks natural and unplanned, much thought and care has gone into creating this path.

Photo courtesy of Bachman's Landscaping Service. Sue Hartley, photography.

This flagstone path wanders directly among the flowers, allowing visitors to enjoy close contact with the garden.

Both photos this page courtesy of Kristine Distel & Associates Landscaping

Here, a meandering path bordered by rocks leads through thick woods, beckoning the curious to stroll softly along its leaf-strewn curves.

BEDS & BORDERS

Beds and borders are most often seen lining the edges within and around your property line. They are built up against houses, fences, sidewalks and walkways as well as around trees. Usually outlined with stone, brick or wood, borders create a definite boundary between the bed and the rest of the yard. Used not only to fill in empty space next to structures, they effectively control erosion and act as an accent to the rest of the yard.

Borders can be filled with any number and variety of plants, from flowers to small shrubs and trees artistically arranged to provide a pleasant blend of color and shape. Small rocks or gravel generally fill in gaps between plants and flowers, although some beds simply contain a large mass of flowers that display a riot of color when in full bloom. When creating a border, think of color and contrast, such as light and dark. Location of flower beds is especially important. Research the amount of sun and type of climate plants and flowers do best in before you plant to save expense and heartache later.

This terrace has been built in four levels, creating a staggered border that ends at the house. Neatly filled with small rocks in the same neutral color as the wall, the beds have been planted with mums and several varieties of shrubs and small bushes spaced well apart from each other to give them plenty of growing room.

Photo courtesy of Anchor Wall Systems, Inc.

51

This photo and opposite page courtesy of Bachman's Landscaping Service. Sue Hartley, photography.

Here a roughly built wall of large field stones creates an attractively casual border for this bed of bright red impatiens.

Vertical landscape timbers curve around this raised bed of annuals and small shrubs, providing a definite boundary between the bed and the walk. A lattice panel behind the border provides an interesting background for the setting and a sense of privacy.

Photo courtesy of Southern Pine Council

A high, terraced retaining wall borders this yard and has been planted with bushes now displaying their brilliant red and yellow fall colors.

Photo courtesy of Anchor Wall Systems, Inc.

This curved gray retaining wall is set off well by the deep green grass below it and the purple, pink and yellow flowers above.

Photo courtesy of Kristine Distel & Associates Landscaping

Red tulips and bright purple hyacinths border this walk, showing their springtime colors and brightening the landscape after winter's duller grays and browns. Bricks line the walk in front, creating a boundary between the flowers and the path.

Solid-colored beds of impatiens and a variety of shrubs, including juniper and flowering spirea, border this sidewalk and soften its edges. They provide color and contrast, not only among themselves, but with the rough textures of stone and brick that make up the walkway.

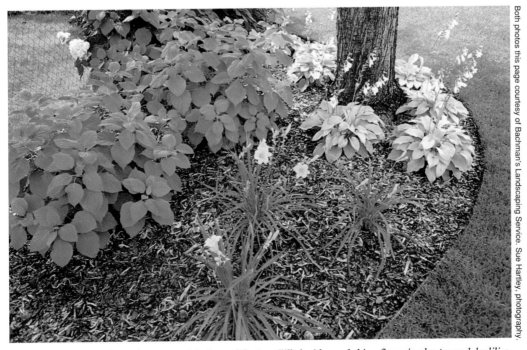

This neat border extends out from around the base of the tree. Filled with wood chips, flowering hostas and daylilies, it creates a soft bed with a quiet and restful appeal.

Both photos this page courtesy of Bachman's Landscaping Service. Sue Hartley, photography.

PLANTERS

Planters are containers in which flowers or smaller plants are grown. They take up much less space than beds, and are attractive because of their distinct shapes as well as their contents. They can be tall or short, of almost any shape and are made from any number of materials, from wood to ceramic. A whole variety of flowers can be grown in planters, where they are often easier to raise. Trailers are a favorite for containers because they hang down over the sides, softening the edges and creating an elegant look. An added benefit of planters is their movability, allowing a change in location either to create diversity in the landscape or to benefit the plant itself.

This square white wooden planter contains a tree rose in full bloom. In cooler climates, container-grown roses need to be treated as annuals.

Photo courtesy of Dundee Nursery

Wooden planters filled with bright begonias line this walk at intervals, creating a blend of textures and colorful red accents that contrast nicely with the subtler tones around them.

Photo courtesy of Jackson & Perkins

Photo courtesy of Western Wood Products Association

Photo courtesy of Osmose Wood Preserving, Inc.

These three wooden planters (above), are really tiers, one built up from the other, and line a matching wooden walkway leading up to a small gazebo. Again, as planters they break up the design of the walkway and are filled with ornamental trees and brightly colored flowers serving as accents to the rest of the landscape.

These built-in planters, filled with begonias and azaleas, line a wooden deck, while smaller flowerpots, easily moved to allow flexibility within the landscape, have been placed alongside them.

GARDENS

For many people, gardens are the spice of life. Whether you have been an avid gardener for years or are just beginning to dabble in the dirt, gardens allow you to bask in the outdoors while enjoying creative fulfillment and the beauty of nature at its best. Both vegetable and flower gardens require work, but even when small in scale, their produce is well worth whatever time and effort was expended on its behalf.

Be judicious in your choice of flowers when planning a flower garden; too many can be overwhelming and will compete against each other for soil and sun. Plant smaller flowers in front and larger ones in back, creating rows that complement each other and blend well together. It is fun to plant with the seasons in mind, so that you have a continual show of flowers for as long as possible. Bulbs such as tulips, daffodils and crocuses start a garden in early spring, while primroses and daisies flower during the summer months and gentians and wintergreen come into bloom in early fall.

Gardens are more than just the flowers, fruits and vegetables they produce. Design, color, layout and even structures need to be considered for a pleasing and productive end result. Notice the different plants, their layout and the use of structures in the gardens that follow.

Annuals, flowers that must be planted anew each year, and perennials, flowers that come back year after year, make up this varied flower bed. Annuals grow faster than perennials and are perfect for large flower beds, flower arrangements and planters and hanging baskets.

Photo courtesy of Dundee Nursery

This elegant formal garden carries an English flavor with its hedges and neat paths. Clipped close, the hedges make up the garden's basic structure while flowers and birdbaths offset their long, green lines. A stone wall surrounds the garden itself, adding another texture and matching the even lines of the hedges to continue the garden's English theme.

Photo courtesy of Terry Tempus, TCT Landscaping

Rose gardens are often considered the height of both beauty and gardening ability, as can be seen with this small section of roses. Here a birdbath rests in the middle of an array of rose bushes while a flagstone path wanders among them, broadening the garden's use and allowing closer contact with its flowers.

Photo courtesy of Jackson & Perkins

An artful trellis supports climbing roses, a myriad of petunias and rose bushes surrounding its base. The unique design of the trellis goes well with the jumble of color below; together the two create a beautiful and original garden scene.

Photo courtesy of Kristine Distel & Associates Landscaping

Beds of tulips and yellow daffodils grace this garden in early spring. The first flowers to emerge after a long and cold winter, they promise that warmer days will follow.

TREES & SHRUBS

Trees and shrubs are useful in landscapes for many reasons. They provide shelter and shade, protect the soil, serve as windbreaks and create physical barriers that act as screens, preventing unwanted traffic and controlling noise. They also provide beauty and are a valuable contribution to the conservation of our planet.

When choosing trees and/or shrubs for your landscape, you must first of all be aware of the different kinds of trees (conifer, deciduous, evergreen and palm) and which grow best in your climate. Walk around the neighborhood noting different types of trees in the yards around you, and visit a local nursery to discuss which types of trees are best suited to your locale. A good nursery can also tell you which trees are hardiest and where and how they should be planted.

When you have determined how many and what kind of trees you want, put your plan on paper. Draw a rough design that includes each tree, noting wind direction and amount of available sun throughout the day as well as spacing between trees and other areas of the landscape. Trees and shrubs are an important and expensive investment in your landscape and should be chosen and planted with care.

These shrubs, bushes and trees have been planted to create contrast in the landscape by careful use of differing textures, shapes, sizes and colors. Use contrast selectively: too many contrasting elements produce a landscape that looks random and unplanned.

Photo courtesy of Bachman's Landscaping Service. Sue Hartley, photography.

Planting a sapling is an investment in the future of the planet and generations to come. When planting a young tree, remember that it will grow, so leave enough open space to accommodate its growth pattern. You can balance a young tree with larger landscaping elements, as can be seen here with the shrubs and retaining wall built behind this young tree.

This graceful stand of white birch screens the side of a house, providing shade and privacy as well as beauty.

All photos this page and opposite page (top) courtesy of Bachman's Landscaping Service. Sue Hartley, photography.

These shrubs and small bushes have been carefully planted well apart from each other, acknowledging future growth. Rocks fill in the gaps between them while a long row of hosta lines the tree behind, adding greenery and depth to the overall landscape.

Photo courtesy of Dundee Nursery

Here a small hedge curves around a stand of bushes, acting both as a barrier and a border. Trees and shrubs can contrast with each other as well as with materials, providing a multitude of textures, colors and shapes.

Hedges make effective barriers without a loss of openness or airflow. Taller hedges protect privacy while providing greenery. Low hedges allow communication with areas beyond your yard. Hedges need to be trimmed and shaped at regular intervals if they are to remain attractive.

VINES & GROUND COVER

Vines are used in conjunction with walls or screens to ensure privacy; mask unsightly fences; soften the hard lines of a fence, wall or house; or simply as additional climbing plants with a trellis or arbor for support. Generally fast growers, they are perfect as temporary screens or even as longer-lasting additions to the landscape. Vines come in several varieties, many of them flowering, that are worth investigating. Some people claim that no garden is complete without them.

Ground cover is used to cover large areas, often under a tree or along a fence or retaining wall. It is also used, alone or in conjunction with other flowers or plants, to shield an unsightly area. Thickly planted, it can help reduce and even prevent soil erosion on a steep hill. It is also used to soften hard edges, fill in gaps between plants or structures and reduce maintenance in hard-to-reach areas.

Here, cinquefoil covers the base of a retaining wall and is beginning to climb into the crevices between the rocks, filling in the empty spaces with its tiny green leaves and adding color and softness to the scene.

Spreading juniper is a ground-hugging evergreen with prickly needles that is a favorite choice for ground cover. Here it spreads across small rocks on a rise leading up from a retaining wall.

Both photos this page courtesy of Bachman's Landscaping Service. Sue Hartley, photography.

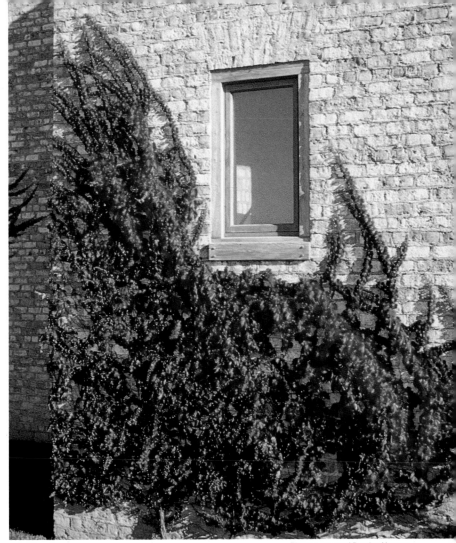

Photo courtesy of Dundee Nursery

Vines are often most striking in the fall, as the flaming red leaves of this ivy show. The contrast between the ivy leaves and the white brick walls of the house is sharp. Keep windows free of vines for an unobstructed view.

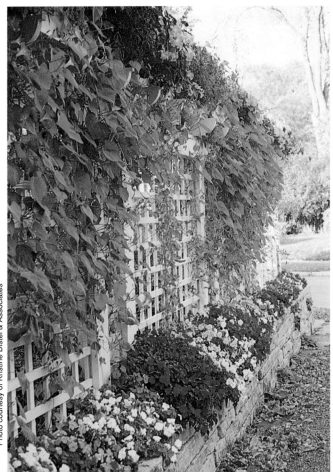

Photo courtesy of Kristine Distel & Associates

Climbing vines need the support of a trellis or similar structure if they are to thrive. Once established, vines require little maintenance although some vines need winter protection in cold climates. Cascading down from flower boxes atop the trellis, flourishing morning glories bear colorful flowers that open each morning with the sun.

FENCES, WALLS & GATES

Fences and walls are used to enclose a yard either partially or completely in order to provide definition, security and privacy. They are an effective barrier to unpleasant sights and sounds, and act as a deterrent to trespassers of all ages and sizes. They also block strong winds and unpleasant weather.

Depending on their height and the type of material used for construction, fences and walls send a message to others about what lies within. High, solid walls keep people from peering inside and offer a great deal of privacy. Low or partial walls make your property visible while still serving as a boundary, thus allowing others to enjoy your landscape without intruding.

Fences and walls should integrate with the rest of your landscape, including the house. They also need to be compatible with the neighborhood, so note these types of structures in the yards around you. They can be made from brick, stone or various types and styles of wood, as well as from a row of plants or even trees planted closely together. Stone walls store heat from the sun during the day and radiate it back at night, which makes them ideal for heat-loving plants. Screens and latticework let in light and air, maintaining a connection with the rest of the environment as they create enclosures. Certain areas limit how high you are allowed to build your fence, so check zoning codes before beginning construction.

Gates are a necessary part of fences and walls, serving as a point of entry and exit. They can either blend in with the rest of the fence, in which case they should be of the same or similar material and color, or they can be distinctive and clearly defined. Bright colors and additional trim, such as arches or vines, are ways to heighten a gate and make it an individual part of the wall.

A small trellis above the doorway, made from the same redwood as the fence, sets off this simple iron gate, making this point of entry noticeable and inviting. The gate's open grillwork relieves the severe nature of the fence and provides a pleasant connection between the interior and the exterior of the yard.

Photo courtesy of California Redwood Association

Photo courtesy of Osmose Wood Preserving, Inc. Opposite page, top photo courtesy of Bachman's Landscaping Service. Sue Hartley, photography.

Here a small picket fence acts more as a border than a barrier, announcing the edge of the yard without fuss. Flowers and climbing plants go well with the fence, creating a small-town atmosphere and a sense of summer's ease.

Latticework tops this high fence, softening its impenetrable face and adding a touch of elegance to a barrier that is clearly not to be crossed.

Photo courtesy of Norby & Associates, Inc.

A wooden fence lines this pool, providing privacy for swimmers and sunbathers inside. Pools can be dangerous to unsupervised children and animals, so the fence becomes a safety feature as well.

This low stone wall forms an attractive boundary between two distinct areas within the landscape, separating them without blocking the view. Pink mums at the base of the wall add color and soften the stone's harsher lines.

Photo courtesy of Terry Tempus, TCT Landscaping

A low retaining wall made of limestone divides a sloped yard into two different areas. Plantings along both sides of the wall help to blend it naturally into the landscape.

This wall, made of decorative cement blocks in an attractive pattern and with a pleasantly rough texture, serves as a solid, well-built boundary around the edge of the yard.

Photo courtesy of Bachman's Landscaping Service. Sue Hartley, photography.

These three sections of fencing, set several feet apart, are the focal point in this landscape, providing definition as well as artistic style.

TRELLISES, ARBORS & GAZEBOS

Trellises, arbors and gazebos are structures that add extra interest to your yard, especially when covered with vines or climbing plants. A trellis is a lightweight frame of latticework used specifically to support climbing plants; an arbor is simply a bower or open canopy covered with plants and used to provide shade. When built next to the house, an arbor is useful as a transition area and also serves to screen sun and wind. A gazebo is a permanent structure reminiscent of a tiny house with one or more open sides. It can serve as a dining area, a protected sitting space or a private retreat.

Structures such as these are wonderful additions to the landscape but need to be considered carefully. Usually made out of wood, they should blend with the rest of the yard, as well as the house. Scale them appropriately or they'll take over the landscape. A small arbor covered with wisteria or a gazebo tucked among the trees can be enchanting.

Teakwood Garden Furniture by Barlow Tyrie

Shade filters down on benches beneath this arbor while the vines surrounding it provide additional protection and privacy. This arbor cunningly rests on trellises, with the entire structure built as one piece and providing a pleasant seating area.

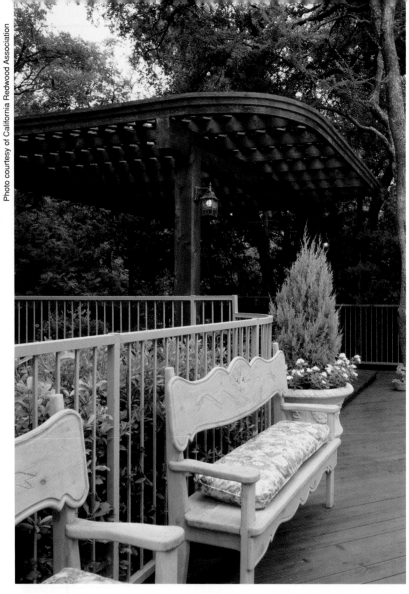

Photo courtesy of California Redwood Association

The beauty of this arbor (left) lies in the design and redwood used for its construction; plants would only hide its character. Covering a walkway, the arbor is a ceiling, screening the sun and weather.

Vines drop down between the slats (below), while sunlight and shade create contrasting patterns, as seen from the underside of this intricately constructed arbor.

Photo courtesy of Southern Pine Council

Photo courtesy of Kristine Distel & Associates Landscaping

A white trellis supports morning glories that fill a wide planter built on top, doubling as a barrier or wall with slats. Impatiens fill a stone bed that borders the trellis, the two features working well together both structurally and as flower beds.

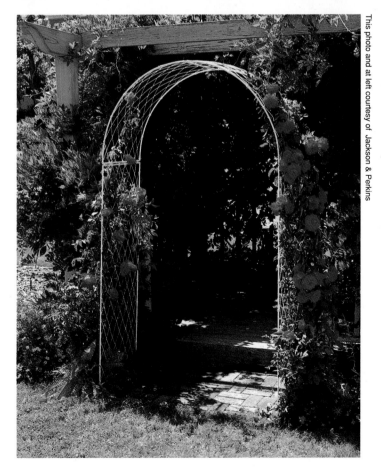

This photo and at left courtesy of Jackson & Perkins

The unique designs of these unusually constructed trellises and arbors are heightened by the elegance of climbing vines. One offers a novel seating area and the other serves as a point of entry into a mysterious garden.

Photo courtesy of California Redwood Association

Sporting a tiered and pointed roof, this redwood gazebo is open on all sides, extending an invitation to rest in its shade. Vines and plants surround the gazebo, acting as living walls and enclosing the area in cool, green growth.

Photo courtesy of Norby & Associates, Inc.

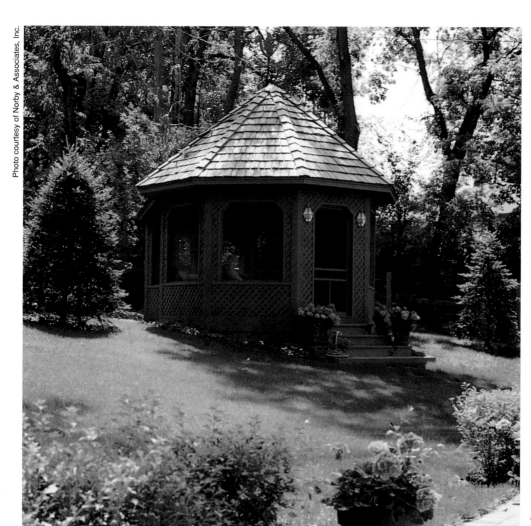

Looking like a small house with open windows, a shingled roof, potted geraniums in the doorway and exterior lights to point the way in the dark, this gazebo could come from a fairytale, like a candy house in the woods.

Photo courtesy of Southern Pine Council

This gazebo features 2 × 2 wood-framed sides made of treated Southern Pine that act as screens, providing a buffer against the weather and shade from the sun. This gazebo acts like a small summer house with four sides and a door; the open walls let in the breeze and sweet smells of summer.

LIGHTING

The purpose of lighting in your landscape is twofold; first, to illuminate, and second, to serve as a safety feature. In addition, lighting adds an artistic touch. Whether by choosing unique fixtures or by illuminating far corners on a dark and rainy night, using light in your landscape adds an element of mystery, magic and romance.

As with other areas you will consider when landscaping, it is important to plan your use of lighting before installing it, and this plan should be based on your overall design. Note areas where unattractive and harsh light already exists and see if you can replace it with something softer. Consider highlighting an attractive feature, such as a certain plant, statue or fountain.

If safety is an important issue, a bright light in your yard will deter intruders. Colored lights around the deck add a festive element to outdoor entertainment.

Walk around your yard at night and note areas that already receive light, whether from the street or a neighbor's house. Imagine how light, strategically placed, would change the effect and add to your existing vision. It is also important to consider where you will be installing lights and burying lines. Make certain your plans conform to local codes.

Light surrounds this multilevel deck as twilight darkens the sky. Fixtures have been placed at intervals along the tiers and encircle the main area of the deck itself, not only providing an accent to the night, but offering security.

Photo courtesy of Bachman's Landscaping Service. Sue Hartley, photography.

Sunlight gives this fountain a pale sparkle during the day while the same water at night, lit from within, takes on a surreal glow. Various fixtures around the walkway and within and without the house work together with the fountain to illuminate the entire area.

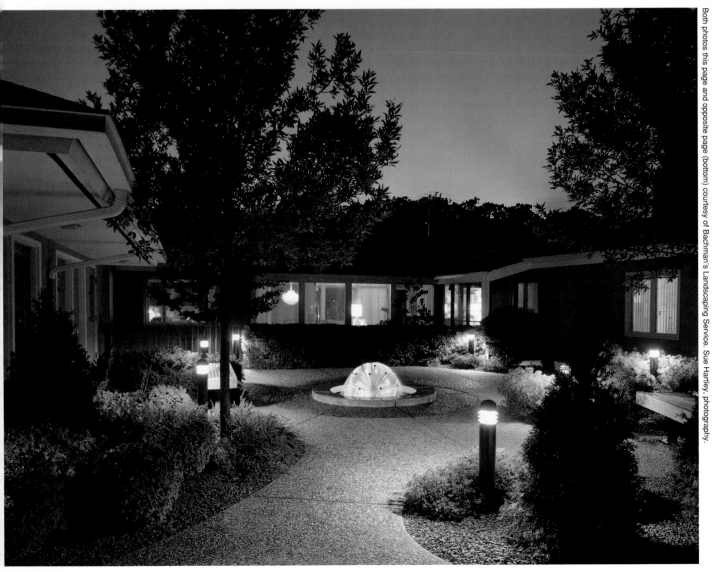

Both photos this page and opposite page (bottom) courtesy of Bachman's Landscaping Service. Sue Hartley, photography.

Photo courtesy of Liteform Designs

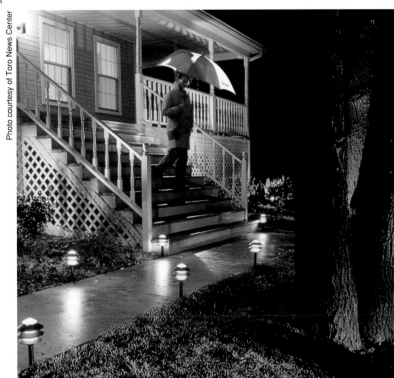

Photo courtesy of Toro News Center

Standing at attention like sentinels, these various fixtures guard their posts, casting light along the path to show the way.

Two large lamps set on pillars across from each other spread their light over the front of this house, brightening the landscape and highlighting the red of the bricks in the walk and the flowers alongside it. Extra light on the ground and the garage add to the expanse of light that covers the area.

PORTFOLIO

This photo and photo at bottom left courtesy of Bachman's Landscaping Service. Sue Hartley, photography.

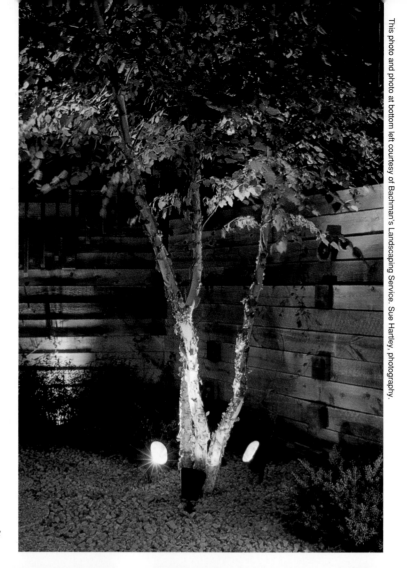

Here a tree stands illuminated by ground-level lamps while shadows from the corner wall near which it is planted bounce off the wood and run along the rocks.

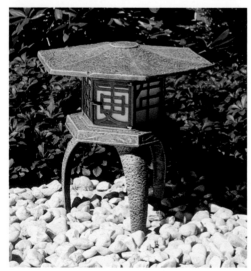

This small Chinese light fixture looks like an unusual sculpture, creating a focal point in the landscape during the day and providing light at night.

Snapdragons, marigolds and impatiens are lit by this small light in front, their colors looking all the more brilliant in the gleam.

Photo courtesy of Classic & Country Crafts

Photo courtesy of Doner Design, Inc.

This curved, weathered flower fixture, complete with bent leaves, blends with a bed of irises while, opposite, a whimsical mushroom light adds a humorous touch to the landscape.

This photo and opposite page (bottom right) courtesy of Hanover Lantern

Photo courtesy of Classic & Country Crafts

A small square light (above), set off by a peaked roof, looks like a house filled with tiny glass windows.

An iron hanging lamp (left), spreads its glow against a brick background.

SPECIAL FEATURES

Water, Ponds & Pools

      Water can be used as an accent, as with a small pond or stream, or for activity, as with a swimming pool. Both the sight and the sound of water add an attractive element to a landscape. A still pool of water reflecting shadows from a passing cloud or a babbling brook skipping lightly over rocks create distinctly different impressions that should work with whatever other elements make up the landscape. A spray of water adds sound and activity, as does a bubbling fountain. Even a bird bath brings life to the simplest of landscapes.

      Plants should highlight your use of water, but not detract from it. Depending on the type of design you have created, match plants to the landscape. Place grasses and ferns around a woodland pond, fill a quiet pool with water lilies and surround a marble fountain spraying water with delicate flowers.

Teakwood Garden Furniture by Barlow Tyrie

A wooden bench rests beside a quiet pond, through which goldfish swim beneath the lilies, and reeds at the edge wave in the breeze. The effect is a peaceful retreat where the water soothes, lulling its visitors to sleep.

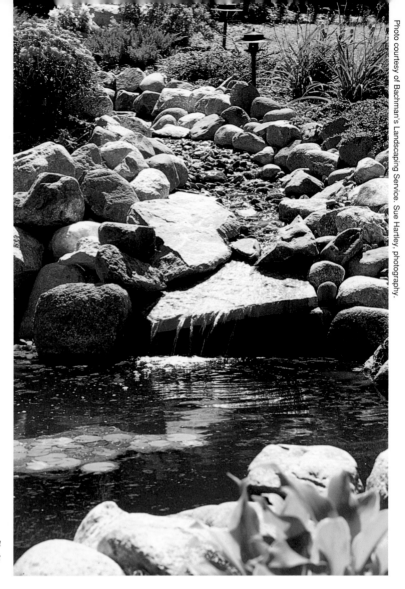

Photo courtesy of Bachman's Landscaping Service. Sue Hartley, photography.

Water flowing down this rocky stream bed enters the pool below with a splash. Although the scene could be taken from a mountain meadow, this stream is part of a larger domestic landscape.

Photo courtesy of Terry Tempus, TCT Landscaping

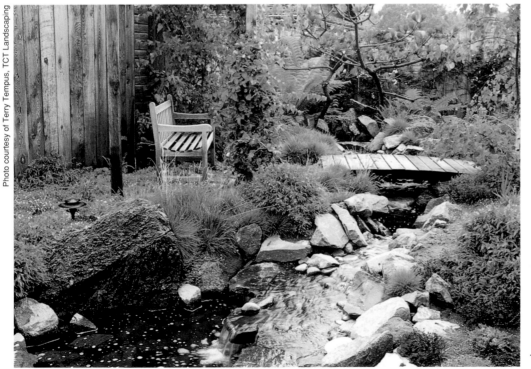

Another bench beside another body of water creates a scene altogether different from the previous one. This landscape has a wakeful tone, with grasses, rocks and vines lying scattered throughout the area and wildlife possibly peering out from the grass. And although this scene, too, looks like it belongs in the wild, the fence behind attests to a human touch.

Photo courtesy of Holm & Olson, Inc.

Hosta, creeping ivy, snapdragons and various other plants encircle this pool, climbing over rocks and shading its sides with their deep green leaves. The pool reflects the sky above and trees branching over its side. A small spray of water pours into the pool, helping to oxygenate the water.

Photo courtesy of Lilypons Water Gardens, Buckeystown, Maryland

Here, a tiny kidney-shaped pool housing lilies and goldfish peeks through flowers and grass like a liquid eye. Tiles and a cement bench border the pool, adding a touch of elegance.

89

SPECIAL FEATURES

Climate

Climate has a direct impact on your landscape. Factors such as sun, rain, snow, fog, wind, humidity and even city smog will affect your choice of trees, shrubs, plants and flowers. Research your area so you are familiar with the type of climate you live in, and peruse gardening books to determine which plants do best in your area.

Gardens do best when adapted to the climate. Remember that the number and length of seasons where you live will determine how much time you will be spending outside. Coastal regions can be either balmy and mild or windy and cold; southern states have longer growing seasons and plants easily survive their mild winters; places with lots of cold should consider hardier plants, trees and bushes as well as structures that look attractive bare of leaves and covered with snow.

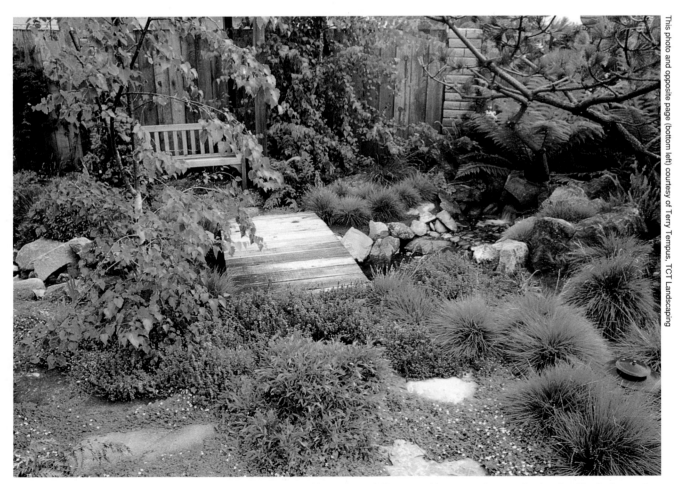

This photo and opposite page (bottom left) courtesy of Terry Tempus, TCT Landscaping

Untrimmed grass and various other plants lie scattered throughout this garden in full summer bloom, growing together in a jumble of colors and uneven textures.

Photo courtesy of Western Wood Products Association

Summer sunlight bakes this deck, making it perfect for sunbathing or just relaxing. Pillows and a wicker chair with umbrella overhead create a comfortable resting place. Decks such as these are ideal for hot, sunny climates.

Photo courtesy of Bachman's Landscaping Service. Sue Hartley, photography.

Evergreens leave a carpet of needles watered by a sprinkler, an essential source of water in drier climates. Hardy trees such as these grow throughout the continent and are at home in a variety of landscapes.

Rather than trying to grow lush fields in a dry climate, this landscape uses blue fescue, an ornamental grass that grows in tufts, planted around a rocky outcrop. Other native plants surround the grass and complete the desert scene.

SPECIAL FEATURES

Extra Elements

Extra features and unusual items add the finishing touch to a landscape. They include unique and unusual shapes, colors and groupings that make an interesting landscape extraordinary.

The pictures that follow display items with distinctive traits and characteristics that point to the individuality of the one who installed them and add an extra element of creativity to each scene.

This photo and opposite page (top) courtesy of California Redwood Association

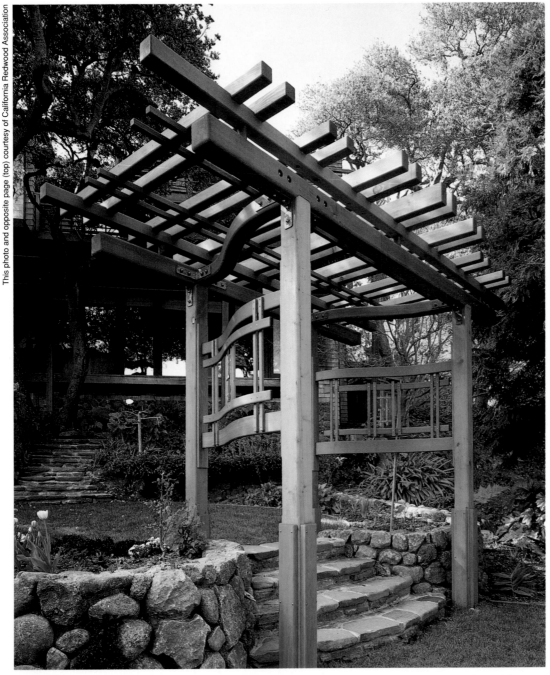

This distinctive pagoda-like redwood structure is a major focal point and gives the rest of the garden an Oriental theme which is carried out in the plants, flowers and other elements.

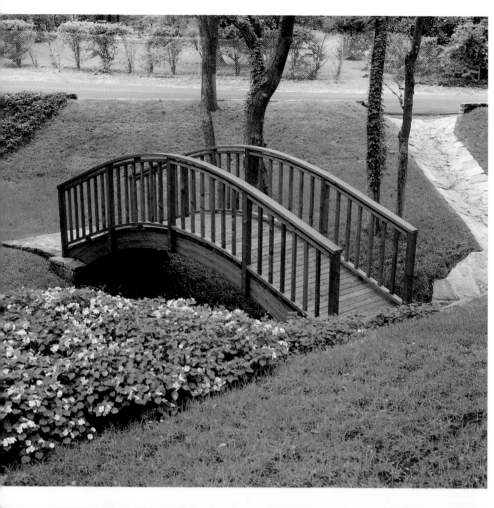

An arched redwood bridge spans an empty stone drainage ditch used for run-off from the street beyond. The bridge and bed of impatiens next to it add beauty to a scene usually considered unattractive.

Photo courtesy of Norby & Associates, Inc.

A bubbling fountain surrounded by pink geraniums adds a perfect touch to this small brick courtyard.

Photo courtesy of Bachman's Landscaping Service. Sue Hartley, photography.

Here an ordinary birdbath rests beneath a tree and inside a bed surrounded by geraniums and juniper. The bath and birds it attracts add flair to this small landscape.

Teakwood Garden Furniture by Barlow Tyrie

A wooden bench cleverly encircles this broad tree, creating a comfortable and attractive resting place beneath the tree's branches.

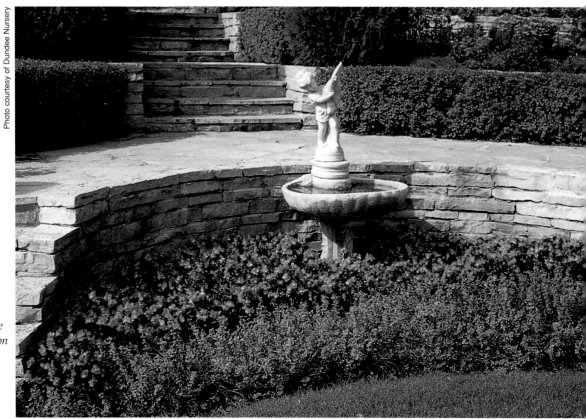

Photo courtesy of Dundee Nursery

A fountain resting inside the curve of a combination stone retaining wall and walkway doubles as a birdbath and rises up grandly among a bed of pink begonias.

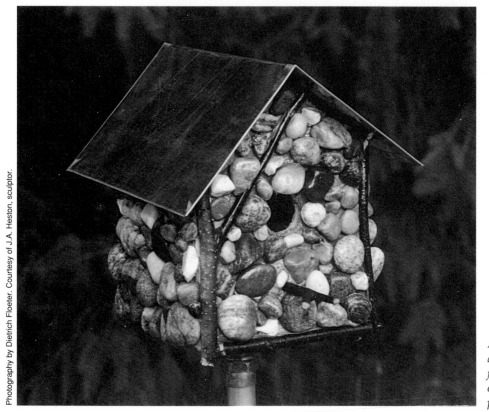

Photography by Dietrich Floeter. Courtesy of J.A. Heston, sculptor.

A simple birdhouse made of stones, with a copper roof and twigs for beams, blends form and function. The house will not only be a home for birds but will add personality to the scene.

LIST OF CONTRIBUTORS

We'd like to thank the following companies for providing the photographs used in this book:

Anderson Design Services, Ltd.
P.O. Box 5264
Minnetonka, MN 55343-2264
(612) 473-8387

Anchor Wall Systems
8309 Brooklyn Blvd.
Brooklyn Park, MN 55445
For the number of the nearest manufacturer
and the availability of Anchor Diamond,
Anchor Windsor Stone and Anchor Sahara Stone,
call Anchor Wall Systems at (800) 473-4452.

Bachman's Landscaping Service
6010 Lyndale Ave. S.
Minneapolis, MN 55419
(612) 861-7600

Barlow Tyrie Inc.
1263 Glen Ave., Suite 230
Moorestown, NJ 08057
(609) 273-7878

California Redwood Association
405 Enfrente Drive, Suite 200
Novato, CA 94949
(415) 382-0662

Classic & Country Crafts
5100-1B Clayton Rd., Suite 291
Concord, CA 94521
(510) 672-4337

Kristine Distel & Associates Landscaping
1844 Glenwood Pkwy.
Golden Valley, MN 55422
(612) 751-0377

Doner Design, Inc.
2175 Beaver Valley Pike
New Providence, PA 17560
(717) 786-8891

Dundee Nursery & Landscape Co.
16800 Hwy. 55
Plymouth, MN 55446
(612) 559-4004

Handcrafted Copper & Stone Sculpture
9796 West Bay Shore Drive
Traverse City, MI 49684
(616) 947-5259

Hanover Lantern
470 High St.
Hanover, PA 17331
(717) 632-6464

Holm & Olson
159 Duke St.
St. Paul, MN 55102
(612) 222-0521

Jackson & Perkins
Medford, OR 97501
(800) 854-6200

Lilypons Water Gardens
6800 Lilypons Rd.
P.O. Box 10
Buckeystown, MD 21717-0010
(800) 723-7667

Liteform Designs
P.O. Box 3316
Portland, OR 97208
(503) 257-8464

Kevin G. Norby & Associates, Inc.
10901 Red Circle Drive, Suite 125
Minnetonka, MN 55343
(612) 938-0020

Osmose Wood Preserving, Inc.
P.O. Drawer O
Griffin, GA 30224-0249
(800) 241-0240

Southern Pine Marketing Council
2900 Indiana Ave.
Kenner, LA 70065
(504) 443-4464

TCT Landscaping
2209 Green St.
Cambria, CA 93428
(805) 927-3950

Toro News Center
1401 W. 76th St., Suite 420
Minneapolis, MN 55423
You may contact Toro News Center
for a free lighting brochure.

Western Wood Products Association
Yeon Bldg., 522 S.W. 5th Ave.
Portland, OR 97204-2122
(503) 224-3930